Notes

Book to
Read to
Edna y Luke
Weaver

The Messiah Child

❡

Written and Illustrated

Jean E. Lobb-Fries
Copyright Library of Congress, 1992

ISBN: 1974654079
ISBN 13: 9781974654079

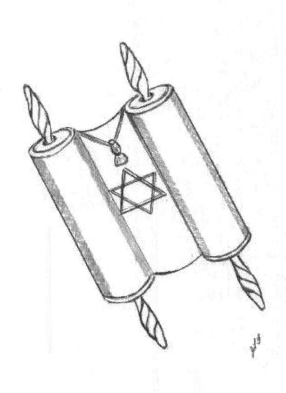

Table of contents

Introduction

§

I REALIZE THAT THE BIBLE doesn't say much about the childhood of the Messiah so this is a fictional account of facts that I have gleaned from other sources such as The Archko Volume by Rev. W.D. Mahan, first copyrighted in the year 1887 by Keats Publishing, Inc. Two men, Doctors McIntosh and Twyman translated from the ancient archeological writings of the Sanhedrim and Talmuds of the Jews legal documents that they found in two very secure locations. These were documents that had been carefully preserved over the centuries. These are eyewitness reports by the priest in the temple of Bethlehem, Herod's report, and Pilate's report to Rome, as well as those who were sent by the Sanhedrim to verify or deny the claims of some that the Messiah was not killed in the massacre of the babies of Bethlehem. The NIV Study Bible was also used as a source. Some Bible quotations are from the Holy Bible, New International Reader's Version (NIrV) published by Biblica, Inc. 1998.

Jesus always knew who he was, an eternal being living in an earthly body. He gave us a visual example of what we can become as children of God.

May this story bring to life the wonderful Messiah, the son of man, who grew up among us and revealed Himself to be the Son of Almighty God, the Creator of the universe.

CHAPTER 1
Bethlehem of Judea

§

"JAKE, WAKE UP! WAKE UP! The sky is exploding!

The young shepherd was shaking and could hardly speak for the fear that gripped his heart. Something was happening that looked to him like the end of the world.

"Wha...what's the matter, Joe?"

Jake was sleepily rubbing his eyes. He hadn't been asleep more than an hour. His watch to take care of the sheep was later that night, more toward morning, and he needed the sleep to be able to handle the responsibility of caring for the sheep.

"Look! Look! Jake, the sky is exploding with bright lights high up in the heavens and spreading such a brilliant light, it's like daylight out here! Look! It's falling in soft rays across the mountains! You can see the trees and rocks clear as day!"

Jake looked up into the sky and thought he must be still dreaming.

Then all of a sudden, the sky was filled with angels in bright white glistening robes. Some had two wings, some had six wings, some with none at all...suspended in mid air. They were in groups singing and praising God. It was as though a great harp and trumpets and all kinds of musical instruments accompanied them with the most beautiful music that the two shepherds had ever heard.

An angel floated down and told the young shepherds, Jacob and Joseph:

"A wonderful thing has just happened in the city of Bethlehem. God's Son has been born to rule as the King of Righteousness over all the earth.

Don't be afraid, but go over to the stable-cave where you take the sheep when the storms come and there you will find Him in a manger."

Their fear melted into awe, like the glorious fireworks display in the heavens that melted down in brilliant rays over the hillsides, illuminating every rock and crevice.

The sheep were not even spooked by the commotion, but stood, gazing upward as awestruck as the little shepherds.

Time was of no importance at all as they drank in the sight with their eyes and hearts. They were overwhelmed with spontaneous worship as they joined in the wonderful heavenly celebration of the birth of the Messiah, the Lamb of God that was born to take away the sins of the world, whose name in Hebrew is Yeshua, meaning salvation.

"Hey Joe, look, here comes Seth and Zeke running. I bet they saw the same thing we did," shouted Jake.

Seth was ahead of Zeke but because Zeke wanted to be the first one to tell the other two, he put on a burst of speed and raced to Jake and Joe ahead of Seth.

"Hey guys, did you see what we saw?" Zeke exclaimed breathlessly after his hard run to beat Seth.

"Wow! I can't believe it! I'm nobody special. Why would angels want to tell me about God's Son that was just born in Bethlehem? The kids that make fun of me 'cause I'm just an ordinary Bedoin shepherd boy. They will never believe me when I tell them what just happened!"

Zeke was out of breath now after the hard run and the excitement, but before Seth could tell his side of the story, Jake and Joe shouted out together,

"Yes! Yes! We saw everything!"

"Joe and I heard the beautiful music of the angels. The angel of the Lord told us about Him too! I wonder how many others saw what we did."

Jake had no idea of the commotion that was going on at that very moment in Bethlehem. The whole town was serenaded by the heavenly choir and given a display as brilliant as fireworks that woke up and astounded many in the sleepy little town of Bethlehem. They found it hard to believe their eyes and like Joe, thought they must still be dreaming.

"Come on," shouted Joe excitedly, "Let's go over to the stable-cave where the manger is and see him for ourselves."

"But what about the sheep? Who will stay and take care of the sheep? We can't leave them alone because a wild animal would come and take one of them and then how would I explain that to my uncle?"

Zeke thought for a moment and said, "I'll stay for now, but come right back and take my place so I can go and see Him too."

"I'll be back as soon as I can Zeke." The desert dust rose in a quick cloud under Joe's sprinting feet.

The other three shepherds rushed off toward the cave where the angel had told them to find the baby who was sent from heaven but who was just like them.

CHAPTER 2

Commotion in Bethlehem

§

MELKER, A PRIEST IN BETHLEHEM, was in the synagogue praying at the moment the sky burst forth with lights and music. Running out into the street he gazed up into the night sky. His first reaction was fear and then amazement at the wonderful sight. "Is this how it all ends?!" he spoke his thoughts out loud.

Melker had studied the Scriptures all his life and was especially interested in prophecies concerning the Messiah. He had even determined through prophetic visions and revelations given to the prophets Ezekiel, Daniel and Micah, that the Messiah would soon come to Israel.

It was as though, somehow, he had been expecting something like this to happen.

"He's here! He's here, somewhere in Bethlehem! I know he's here." Melker was beside himself with excitement and his shouts began to wake up sleepy heads.

"This is wonderful! This is what the Bible prophesied would happen...right here in our little town of Bethlehem, the city of David."

People began poking groggy heads out their windows, looking down at the priest in his robes shouting and jumping with his hands pointed up to the sky. Then their aggravation at being awakened turned to awe as they noticed the daylight brightness of the sky and the beautiful music coming from it.

Their mouths fell open in awe as they realized that this was a heavenly display honoring someone wonderful. Melker's wife poked out of her second story bedroom window at her husband dancing in the street.

"What in the world is going on?" she shouted. But her aggravation turned to fear as she thought that surely God was bringing the world to an end.

Melker saw her and put his finger to his lips, "Listen, the angels of God are singing about the Messiah."

The angels had not told the townspeople where to find the baby, who was born the King of the Jews, like they told the shepherds.

Bethlehem was crowded with people from all over Israel who belonged to the family of King David. There wasn't a vacant room in the local inn. Surely someone that important would be in a special house. No one even guessed that it was the stable.

It was because of the census and taxation that Caesar Augustus, the Roman Emperor, had commanded.

Everyone had to register in the town that corresponded with their particular family. For Mary and Joseph it was the town of Bethlehem, the City of David.

Melker knew Micah's prophecy, Micah 5:2:

"But you, Bethlehem Ephrathah, though you are small among the clans of Judah, out of you will come for me one who will be ruler over Israel, whose origins are from of old, from ancient times." (NIV)

He also knew Isaiah's prophecy about the Messiah. Isaiah 7:14:

"Therefore the Lord himself will give you a sign: the virgin will be with child and will give birth to a son, and will call Him Immanuel, (meaning God with us)." (NIV)

The shepherds were nearly out of breath from running all the way from the fields to the stable where they were told to go by the angels.

The stable was little more than a shed projecting out from the side of the hill at the cave entrance.

They stood in motionless wonder as they gazed at the small room lit with a heavenly glow. They were speechless as they looked at the beautiful young woman with her precious child. Joseph was resting off to one side.

Mary smiled and invited them to come over and look at his face.

"His name is Yeshua (Jesus) which mean salvation," she said softly.

They could hardly believe that she would allow them to come so close to this wonderful One whose birth had been celebrated and announced by angels.

Joseph motioned to them invitingly, smiling, "Come closer."

The tiny Savior of the world was nestled comfortably in His mother's arms, blinking His eyes and moving His head in the direction of the shepherds.

"Do you think He can see us, ma'am?" asked Seth. "We came as soon as we could after the angels told us where to find Him."

The baby Jesus turned His head toward Seth as though He knew what he had just said.

"Did you see that Joe? He smiled at me!"

The little stable was glowing with the heavenly light of the presence of God. Mary sat and thought about all the things that the shepherds told her and thought how very blessed she was to have been chosen by God to bring the Savior into the world. She knew that it was not because of her goodness but because of God's love and grace that she had been chosen. She was also a descendant of King David, which fulfilled the prophetic scriptures.

The young shepherds from the hillsides came and went throughout the night in shifts.

They quickly spread the news of this wonderful night, the night when God celebrated the birth of His Son.

They were eyewitnesses. They would tell and retell the story throughout the rest of their lives.

Some would believe their story and some would not.

CHAPTER 3

Wise Men Seek Him

§

MATTHEW 2:1-12

IT SEEMED NO TIME AT all before the sun came up that morning and shed its bright rays into the little stable, warming up the straw on which the little baby lay bundled in the strips of linen especially prepared for Him.

Meanwhile, Melker, the priest in Bethlehem, had been excitedly running through the streets, waking up his fellow priests and Rabbis to tell them of the wonderful things that he had seen and heard. Because he had diligently studied the Scriptures concerning the Messiah's birth, he was convinced that the Messiah was indeed there in Bethlehem, born that night of a virgin...but where, he didn't know.

In the predawn darkness he and his friends gathered in the street. Now as the dawn was breaking over the eastern sky, suddenly, two very excited shepherd boys came running toward them.

"It was awesome! Totally awesome!" shouted one of the boys.

Melker shouted back, "Where is He? Did you see Him?

"Yes! We saw Him! He's over there in the stable on the edge of town. I can't believe it! God let me see Him and even told me where to find Him through His holy angels."

While the boy was still talking, Melker and his friends began running toward the stable at the edge of town.

"Oh, hallelujah! Praise Jehovah God! He kept His promise to us and sent us the One who will save us from our enemies and set up His kingdom over all the earth!"

Melker was so excited that he stumbled and ran haltingly over the cobblestone street, the fringe on his long priestly robe catching on the stubble of twigs that lay strewn over the street.

When he arrived at the entrance of the cave which had been made into a stable, he fell on his face before Mary and the Baby and worshipped God. The brilliant glory of God lit up the dingy smelly stable, turning it into a cathedral of beauty.

"Please, may I have the honor of your coming to my house?" Melker's words spilled out as he was catching his breath from the hard run.

"Bethlehem is so crowded at this time. I am so sorry that my Lord was forced to be born in a humble stable. He deserves the silk of royalty, but God in His wisdom chose this humble place. If it would please you and God, I beg you to please come and stay at my home for as long as you need."

Mary and Joseph had very little with them, so it didn't take long for them to gather up their things and follow Melker to his home.

They stayed there for a few days. Each day, Melker brought people in and showed them by the Scriptures that this child, indeed, was the promised Messiah.

Word began to spread all across Judea by the mouths of the shepherd boys and the priests who had come to see Him that magnificent night. Even the king, Herod the Great, had been told these rumors.

The next morning after arriving at the house, there was heard a commotion of camels and strange voices in the distance coming up the hillside toward the house of Melker. Joseph went outside to see what was going on.

Three very elegantly dressed men had arrived, one with a long, flowing, purple silk robe with sashes of yellow and green. After bowing his face to the ground in reverent greeting, he introduced himself to Joseph.

People called these strange people Magi or Wise Men. These people called Magi were priests and teachers and followers of Zoroaster, that embraced the books and the Law of Moses. They studied carefully the prophetic Scriptures concerning the coming Messiah.

There was a great crowd of people travelling with them…family, servants, camels and other animals.

"Kind sir," the dark skinned one said, "God directed each of us by dreams to come and present our gifts and our lives to this Great One who is born the King of the Jews and Who is destined to rule over all people and nations forever. We all had a dream the same night about this. Then a great star appeared in the eastern sky, and guided us to this place. See, it is still shining even though it is now day!"

Joseph listened in amazement as they told how they had met at the crossroads, each one of them bringing a special gift for the King of the Jews who was the Child of promise.

Joseph brought them in. When they saw the baby Jesus, after removing their turbans from their heads, they bowed themselves down to the earth.

Arising, they motioned to their servants to bring in the treasure chests. They brought many things, but the gifts that God had instructed them to bring were gold, frankincense and myrrh, which they softly laid at the feet of Mary and the baby Jesus.

For some of them, it had taken two years to get there from the time that the star appeared unto them in the heavens and the Lord told them to go to the land of Israel where they would find this Savior of the world, the king of the Jews.

The wise man from Egypt spread out soft cushions on the ground and invited Joseph to come and chat as he explained their strange mission.

"You see, Joseph, it was quite natural for us to believe that the king over Israel, Herod Antipater, would certainly be aware of what was happening in his own country. But when we inquired of him in Jerusalem as to where to find this One who was born the king of the Jews, he didn't seem to know much about it.

"He could not believe our story and tried to tell us we were all mistaken. So he asked some of his counselors about the prophecies concerning the Messiah and they told him that the child would be from Bethlehem, the city of David. He even asked us to come back and let him know where he could be found so that he too could come and worship him."

That night was a night of celebration for the visitors who came such a long way to find this one that God had told them about.

They celebrated with music and dancing in the oriental customary way, and brought some offerings of sweet dates and honey cakes for this little family. The excitement that His birth had brought to that little town of Bethlehem was no small thing.

The Magi celebrated each day for several days and the townspeople joined in the joy of this wonderful thing that came to their little town.

They put up their tents and lay down for the night.

As they slept the angel of the Lord gave each of them the same dream. They had to leave immediately by another way and not return to tell King Herod where the child was.

The Magi had no way of knowing the cruel intent of the evil heart of King Herod, but they knew that they had heard from God and packed up their things and left immediately.

Joseph was also warned by an angelic visitor in the night by a dream. He must take Mary and the baby to Egypt immediately. First though, he had to take the baby boy to Jerusalem to the temple for his circumcision, for now he was eight days old.

The joy of the birth of the King, the Messiah, in Bethlehem would soon turn to loud cries of sorrow as the evil king Herod planned to quell all this talk about a "King of the Jews" born in Bethlehem.

CHAPTER 4
The Foolish Wicked King

§

MATTHEW 2:1-8, 16-18

BACK IN JERUSALEM, HEROD ANTIPATER, also known as Herod the Great, frantically tried to quell the excitement of the people that the Messiah had come. He had been appointed king over Israel's province of Judea by the Roman government and saw these rumors as threats to the Roman authority and his rule...in particular.

"These superstitious Jews, will they never cease to annoy me with their constant babbling about this invisible God's book?! Why can't they be reasonable and have gods they can see and carry with them? All this nonsense about music and noises from heaven that the priest Melker and those shepherd boys heard is bringing this city to the brink of anarchy against the Roman authority."

Herod turned red with rage as he cursed and vowed to put an end to these rumors once and for all.

"They just don't want to pay taxes! Yes, that's it! It's their way of getting out of it," he shouted.

"It's an insurrection! All the children of Bethlehem and Jerusalem are stirring it up! I have to put an end to this, NOW!"

While Herod raged in Jerusalem, in Bethlehem, the three Magi and their people were heading home by a different route.

Mary and Joseph quickly started out on their journey to Jerusalem for Yeshua's ritual circumcision, according to the Law of Moses. (Yeshua is the Hebrew name for Jesus.) From there they would head off to Egypt.

Herod did not know that Mary, Joseph, and the Messiah child were right there in Jerusalem when he called his soldiers together and gave them orders to go into Bethlehem and kill all the babies who were two years old and younger.

As Mary and Joseph brought the baby into the temple for His circumcision, the thundering hooves of soldier's horses were heard as they headed out of Jerusalem toward Bethlehem.

Only a week before, Bethlehem had witnessed the most magnificent sight ever beheld by human eyes...God's celebration of the birth of his Son, as foretold by the prophets.

Their joy soon turned to cries of sorrow as another prophecy was fulfilled by the murder of all the baby boys two years old and younger.

Simeon, the elderly temple priest, knew that the Christ child would be brought into the temple for His circumcision when he was eight days old. He too, had heard the stories of the shepherd boys who witnessed the magnificent heavenly celebration in Bethlehem, just eight days ago.

Because of this, he came to the temple early that morning, hoping to see Him. The Lord had promised him that he would not die until his eyes would behold the Christ.

When he saw the Baby Jesus in His mother's arms the Spirit of the Lord revealed to him that this was the One he had been looking for.

He tenderly requested permission and lifted Him up before God saying:

"Lord, you are the King over all. Now let me, your servant, go in peace. That is what you promised. My eyes have seen your salvation. You have prepared it in the sight of all people. It is a light to be given to those who aren't Jews. It will bring glory to your people Israel." (Luke 2:29-32 NIrV)

While Mary and Joseph were stunned by the declaration of this perfect stranger to them, they knew that God had indeed spoken by the mouth of this man of God.

At that moment, in walked the elderly prophetess, Anna. She was almost a hundred years old now and had been a widow for eighty-four years.

When she came into the temple, the Spirit of God came upon her and she began to excitedly call to the people around to look at the Baby,

"This is the Redeemer of Israel that we have been waiting for!" Her voice was raised in worship and praise to God.

As some gazed on in silence, others raised their hands and thanked God. Some simply nodded their heads in silence thinking that Anna had spoken out of an unsound, elderly mind.

Mary was still pondering in her heart about the prophecies that Simeon, the Priest, and Anna the Prophetess, had spoken over her son, Jesus.

He was presented to the Lord before the holy altar of God, like a baby lamb which was chosen for its perfection to bear the sins of God's people and the whole world.

No one in Jerusalem was aware of the atrocity taking place in Bethlehem at this same time.

Herod's soldiers tore crying babies and toddlers from their mother's arms, killing them with their merciless swords, as the defenseless parents pleaded and screamed for mercy for their children.

Joseph and Mary learned later about this horrible massacre that took the lives of the baby boys of Bethlehem, and understood why it was so urgent that they leave there and fulfill the prophecy concerning Yeshua and Egypt.

It wasn't easy to leave their home town and start again in a strange land. They had no relatives there. They began to understand how Abraham, their ancestor, had felt when he left his homeland to parts unknown at the urging of the Lord.

They travelled by day and slept by night on their blankets under the stars in a small tent that Joseph built. He had cleverly used his carpenter skills to prepare a sturdy shelter that was collapsible and could be quickly erected to shelter from the desert wind on the long trek to Egypt.

CHAPTER 5

God's Son in Egypt

§

MATTHEW 2:13-15; 2:19-23

AFTER SEVERAL WEEKS OF JOURNEY, the family settled in a small town in Egypt called Mecca, where the family lived during the early years of Jesus' life.

Joseph's carpentry skills provided a comfortable living for the family. Even when Jesus was very young, Joseph taught Him his carpenter trade, but all the while knowing in his heart that He had a destiny far greater than carpentry.

Jesus did everything well. His intelligence and impeccable character gained Him honor and respect at a very early age.

Some of the children noticed that the animals would follow Jesus whenever he walked down the street.

"Here comes Adam with his pets!" the children said jokingly. They didn't know that He was God's son, the last Adam.

Jesus often felt the Father's tug of love in His heart and without saying anything to Mary or Joseph, would walk out the door and down the street toward the field where He would climb His favorite tree and talk with His Father God.

His Father was teaching Him many things from the Scriptures: about the Messiah, His ministry, suffering and ultimate victory over death.

The animals of the field looked forward to His visit and passed the word that He was coming to the tree. Jesus climbed the tree and leaned back with his large soft blue eyes lifted toward Heaven.

A soft song began to come from His lips, a song of love to His Father.

The birds hushed their singing and came closer to listen. The stag from the forest slowly walked over and knelt before Him, resting under the tree.

His mother knew about her son's need to be with His Father and didn't worry about Him. Joseph was sometimes frustrated. It seemed when he wanted to teach Jesus something new the boy just wasn't there.

Jesus had made a good friend with the widow lady, Miriam, who lived on the edge of the village. She was blind and looked forward to the frequent visits of the little child.

"Is that you, my light and love? I've been hoping you would come to visit me today."

Even though her eyes could not see she could see with her heart and sensed a special presence about Him.

The little boy, Jesus, smiled and said, "The beautiful song of the birds is the language that my Father gave them to express their joy to each other and the world."

"Oh, I wish I could see them like you do. I hear their song but I cannot imagine how they must look. I have never seen anything with my eyes, but I can see with my hands." Miriam held out her hands.

Jesus saw a mockingbird in a tree and motioned for it to come to Him. When the bird came down, he perched on the open hand of the young child. He then gently took the bird over to Miriam and put it in her hands.

"The long soft, fuzzy pieces are his feathers. He can fly through the air with his two wings. The mouth of the bird is called the beak. He eats insects, seeds and other small stuff. His feet are thin but real strong with claws that help him to perch on the tree limbs and walk on the ground."

As Jesus spoke, the blind woman felt the bird as it fearlessly held still for her according to the command of the child. She knew in her heart that he was no ordinary child and wondered if this might be the Messiah that had been spoken of by the prophets of ancient Israel Miriam had heard rumors from foreign travelers about someone like that being born in a little town in Israel. But why would he be here in Egypt?

Jesus stayed and talked with Miriam for some time before feeling the tug from His Father God to go home.

Mary stood outside the house calling Jesus to come and eat, but he was nowhere to be found.

One of the children down the street called, "I saw Him going into the meadow in the forest quite some time ago."

Then she knew that His Father had been calling Him to talk to Him, but didn't know that He had gone to visit blind Miriam as well.

Jesus was not aware that He was doing anything that would be considered wrong or disobedient. When He felt the tug of His Father calling to Him, there was no hesitation to answer His call.

As little Jesus walked through the door of the house the family had just finished eating the evening meal. Mary quickly arose and filled Jesus' plate with the lukewarm food.

Joseph looked at Jesus sternly and told Him, "Jesus, we waited for quite a while for you to come home so that we could eat together as a family. It was inconsiderate of you to leave without saying a word to us. Please let this be the last time I have to remind you of this."

"I'm sorry sir," answered Jesus softly. "When my heart tells me to go and be alone with my Father, I don't always stop to think that you or mother may need me too."

Then Jesus excitedly added, as though the matter was now closed, "I showed blind Miriam what a bird looks like today. She sees with her hands. Sometimes when I'm walking and the animals are following me, the children call me Adam. But I think they would like for the animals to like them too."

Joseph's face softened to a smile and all was forgiven.

Mary sat quietly listening. From the very beginning she had stopped trying to figure out how God did things and why. She just pondered them in her heart and observed all that He did and said.

CHAPTER 6
Blessed are the Peacemakers

§

ONE HOT SUMMER DAY, TWO boys were fighting in the street.

"Come on, what did you do with it? My dad made that toy chariot for me and you're just jealous and took it! I'm going to teach you a lesson you won't forget!"

With that the boy grabbed the other boy by the arm and was about to hit him in the face with his fist when Jesus walked up.

"Don't fight! Why would you want your brother to be your enemy? If you're nice to him, he'll be nice to you. Don't you want him to be nice to you?"

The two boys froze with their hands up ready to fight, but at the sound of the voice of Jesus, peace settled over them.

"Who are you to tell us what to do?" The angry boy was surprised by this newcomer.

Jesus looked at him and said, "You left your chariot at your Aunt Rachel's house when the family went to visit yesterday. If you are too quick to accuse someone of wrong-doing, you will be the one in the wrong."

They turned and looked at each other, then back at Jesus. The younger boy asked, "How in the world did you know about our visit to Aunt Rachel's house yesterday?"

Without waiting for a reply the older boy told the younger one, "I'll ask Dad to make one for you too, and we can have chariot races."

The boys turned and thanked Jesus, then ran to their Aunt's house to get the wooden toy chariot.

Jesus was so different in some ways and yet he was just a little boy. He looked and talked like a little boy but his heart had no bad thoughts or desire to do anyone harm.

He loved to be alone with his heavenly Father and learn from Him the truths that would mold his life and future.

It was a hard situation for Joseph, as he didn't fully understand how God was going to use Jesus. He thought that if He were to be the king, he would have to be prosperous to gain the respect of the people. He could not understand a spiritual kingdom that would cover the entire earth.

Nevertheless, Joseph tried to be the parent that he thought God expected him to be and waited to talk to Jesus about His responsibilities to the family and to correct Him for leaving again without saying anything to him or his mother.

As the sun was setting in the west and the sky was painted with fiery orange and pink clouds scattered against the darkening blue sky, Jesus walked through the door.

"Woman! (Jesus lovingly called his mother that), Joseph!" exclaimed Jesus excitedly, "Come out here and look at the beautiful sky that our Father painted for us!"

Mary and Joseph hurried out the door and watched the colors on the clouds change from orange to fuchsia and magenta as the sun sank out of sight behind the black silhouetted mountain.

"Yes, dear, your Father's handiwork is beautiful and new every day. It's there for all His world to see and enjoy. If only they would recognize Him in it. People take His beauty and glory for granted and seldom take time to enjoy it." The words spilled out of Mary as she gazed upward with awe at the beautiful sunset.

Joseph had almost forgotten what he wanted to talk to Jesus about. Then he said, "Jesus, I would like to talk to you inside for a moment," with that serious tone of a parent who has something he feels he has to say but would rather not.

Jesus took his mother's hand and walked into the house with them. Jesus' two smaller brothers, who had been born there in Egypt, were asleep in their beds. They were used to going to bed before dark. James was two and a half years younger than Jesus and Joses was three and a half years younger. God blessed Mary and Joseph's marriage with both boys and girls, but at this time, other than Jesus, there were only James and Joses.

Joseph called Jesus to him and sat him on his knee.

"Jesus," he said, "You need to ask permission of your mother or me before you leave. We are responsible for you and do not want anything to happen that would hurt you."

Jesus looked at him with his large innocent blue eyes, "Joseph," (he never called him father), "you know that I must talk to my Father. He is teaching me all the things that I need to know at this point in my life. He will not allow anything to harm me. His angels walk with me wherever I go."

Joseph looked into the eyes of Jesus and his heart melted with the peace and love that shone from them...such purity and godliness in human form. He took him into his arms and patted his head.

They went into the kitchen where Mary had warmed a glass of goat's milk with a spoon of honey and cinnamon and gave it to Jesus with a hearth cake that she had made from the wheat that she had ground that morning.

She warmed up some tea for herself and Joseph and sat together with Jesus before tucking him into bed.

CHAPTER 7

Growing in Wisdom and Stature

§

LUKE 2:40

AS LONG AS KING HEROD (who had killed the babies in Bethlehem) was alive, Mary and Joseph and their children had to live in exile.

The Egyptian children had to help their parents with the daily chores the same as the Hebrew children. But they also were given time to play and just be children.

They couldn't wait to be with Jesus because he taught them so many things about the creation, and the Creator. Many of their parents did not believe in the one true God, but in idols. Even so the children's hearts were hungry for truth. They knew that something made by human hands could not create the world.

"Jesus, can you talk to us more about God the Father and creation today? We want to know more about Him the way you do! Do you have time today? Please, please…"

The little boy who asked Jesus this was from a wealthy family in town who were idol worshipers.

Jesus said, "You don't know who you are looking for, but because you want truth, you will find Him. You were created in the image of God and you are not complete without Him."

The children chorused, "Yeah, that's right! Tell us more!"

A little girl with a beautiful bronzed face and long black hair hanging down her back past her hips asked, "How can we have Him? He's too big."

Jesus said, "God is a spirit. He's like the wind. It is too big to put in a bottle, but if you open your mouth and face the wind, it will come into your mouth. When you turn your face toward God and open your heart to Him, he will come in. Only He can change the heart."

The children were listening intently when suddenly the mother of one of the children came up and angrily asked, "What are you teaching these children?" She worshipped her goddess, Ashtoreth, and enjoyed the sin that her religion allowed.

"You impudent child!" she angrily said to Jesus. "Who gave you the authority to teach religion to others? I don't want you telling my kid this stuff about a Holy God who created heaven and earth. My god is Ashtoreth and I don't want my kids to think I'm a sinner just because I don't believe the way you do!"

Jesus did not become angry, but He looked her straight in the eye and said,

"You want to believe a lie, but if you teach your child the lie, when he is seeking the truth, you are like a cruel parent who would give a stone to your hungry child who asks for a piece of bread to eat. If you try to keep one of these that God loves from coming to Him, it would be better for you not to have been born, because the consequences for your actions are eternal."

She couldn't say another word. The wisdom with which this child spoke was so final. There was no answer. She took her boy by the arm and yanked him away as the boy cried and pleaded with her all the way,

"Mom, if you'll just listen to Him once, you would know…please let me stay!"

The children each gave Jesus a hug and went their way home, as they thought on the marvelous things they heard from the mouth of this wonderful little Hebrew boy.

CHAPTER 8

Passover Seder

§

LUKE 2:52

THERE WERE OTHER JEWS LIVING in Egypt, but Joseph and Mary longed for their homeland. Egypt was so different. The people were idol worshippers who looked upon the Jews with disdain. Mary and Joseph had fled their homeland in order to save the baby Jesus from the wicked King Herod, who wanted to kill him.

They missed their family and friends whom they had known all of their lives. All of this contributed to the growing sadness and longing for home.

Each year, however, they would return to Jerusalem to keep the feast of the Passover. Each year Jesus went into the temple to listen to the elders and Rabbis teach from the sacred Torah which was the first five books of the Bible written by Moses.

His comments and questions always astounded the teachers for He knew the Scriptures by heart and read the Torah with a distinctive authority.

While in Jerusalem they would stay with friends and relatives who lived near Jerusalem. The Passover Seder was carefully prepared according to the Jewish tradition. The dishes that had been set aside for this once a year occasion would be exchanged from household to household.

It was to be a memorial forever of the salvation of the Lord. All of Israel would remember the night that the death angel came through Egypt, killing the firstborn. But the firstborn children of the families of the Israelites were left safe in their homes because the blood of a spotless lamb was painted on the doorposts of each home.

This final plague, bringing the death of his firstborn son, convinced Pharaoh to let his Hebrew slaves leave Egypt to follow Moses and this powerful God.

Joseph was pondering this scene in his heart as Mary prepared the Passover bread.

"We always use unleavened bread for the Passover dinner because there was no time to let the bread rise, they had to leave in a hurry." Joseph made sure that the children understood why they used the crisp bread that had no leaven.

"Have you ever thought of leaven as sin, Joseph?" asked Jesus. "Maybe the bread without any leaven has a deeper meaning. The manna that our ancestors ate in the wilderness was also without leaven. The Messiah must be offered up as a sinless sacrifice, like the matzah, the unleavened bread.

"Just like bread gives life and strength to those who eat it, the Messiah will give life to those who receive Him."

Mary added, "That's true. No leaven is even allowed in the house for the seven days up to the Passover meal."

Although Mary didn't understand all that was meant by the unleavened bread she held every word that her son said in a special place in her heart.

Jesus continued, "Just as the blood of the lamb had to be applied to the upper cross bar and down the sides of the door, so that the angel of death would pass over, the blood of God's Lamb must be applied to the heart's door to be saved from eternal death."

Both Mary and Joseph looked at Jesus with puzzled amazement. All Israel thought that the Messiah would deliver them from their enemies and set up His kingdom on the earth. They looked forward to freedom from the tyrannical Roman oppression.

They could not comprehend a sinless, suffering Messiah or a spiritual kingdom which would fill the entire earth.

"Where did he learn this?" thought Mary, "I don't understand this. Could this have something to do with what the old priest Simeon, said to me?"

"This child is going to cause many people in Israel to fall and to rise. God has sent him. But many will speak against him. The thoughts of many hearts will be known. A sword will wound your own soul too." (NIrV)

"Son, I don't understand what you mean now but I don't doubt anything you say. The Lord will reveal to us what you mean in His time." Mary's soft comment brought a special peace to everyone there.

Joseph was a very practical man but had little depth of understanding and very little education. His trade as a carpenter had been passed on to him from his father. To be educated, was both expensive and somewhat impractical. To learn to read was really all they considered necessary.

"You better be careful what you say about our traditions, son, or you will make some people angry. The Passover has been given to us by God to remind our people of the miraculous way He delivered them from Egypt." Joseph knew how important the traditions were to his people.

Jesus looked intently into the eyes of Joseph, and spoke with gentle wisdom far beyond his years.

"How can the natural mind understand the mind of God? Hasn't He given you these traditions so that you might recognize the spiritual meaning that each one has in it? They are not simply traditions to remember history but prophetic illustrations to guide you to the truth. Can't you see God's plan for the Messiah in the Passover?"

This reply bothered Joseph because he had never thought of the Passover in any other way than the historical sense.

It was a very sacred tradition which had been carried on for generation after generation.

"That's just what I mean, Jesus. That kind of talk is going to get you and us in a lot of trouble. Everyone knows that the Messiah will deliver us from the hands of our enemies and set up an eternal kingdom to rule the earth.

"It's our destiny and right. I don't remember anywhere where it says that the Messiah will be sacrificed like a Passover lamb. I don't know the Scriptures that well, but I know that this is the opinion of most of the people that I know."

Jesus didn't answer another word. Joseph could not understand.

Mary just hid her son's words in her heart in the special place where she stores them for future reference.

CHAPTER 9

Jerusalem Passover

§

As Mary made the preparations for the long trip back to Jerusalem to celebrate the Passover, she pondered the words of her Son, Jesus. What could he have meant by applying the blood of the Lamb of God to our hearts, like our forefathers did the blood of a lamb to the door posts?

Surely God would not allow any harm to come to His own Son. His son has to rule the kingdoms of the earth.

"I just don't understand what He meant by that." Mary said to herself out loud.

"What are you talking about, Mary?" asked Joseph. "What don't you understand?"

Jesus came in, "Can I help? It's time to go to Jerusalem again, isn't it? I can't wait! This is my favorite time of year."

He looked forward to being with the family, but even more He loved to be in the temple in Jerusalem where He would listen to the reading and discussing of the Torah, the Holy book of God's Word.

It was Mary and Joseph's favorite time of year too. It was a time to be with family and friends that they hadn't seen for a whole year. They could catch up on all the family news…who got married, who died, and who was born.

Passover was celebrated for the entire week but the preparations beforehand took several days as well.

The ingredients for the Passover meal had to be purchased and prepared ahead of time. Which relative they were going to stay with had to be determined.

They soon had everything packed on the animals and set out on their pilgrimage to the sacred city of Jerusalem, the "City of Peace".

Although Jesus was young, He didn't tire easily and was never grouchy with the family. He loved to wait and talk about the various plants and animals and birds that they encountered on the way.

He hadn't attended any school but His knowledge of creatures and plants fascinated those around Him. He always had a way of seeing God's handiwork in everything.

It was springtime and the desert area along the Mediterranean Sea was alive with blossoming trees and baby creatures.

The trip along the seashore was a cooler route than going through the dry Sinai desert. This route also provided opportunity to bathe in the sea. There would be wells and an oasis now and then where they could refresh themselves and the animals.

Jesus was more at home outside than He was in a house. To Him a house was just a place to sleep and eat, but the real living was being with His Father's creation and enjoying His communion and fellowship. As Adam had walked with God in the cool of the garden, Jesus walked with His Father everywhere.

"Look! Did you see that sparrow? She's building her nest. The Father has given her wisdom to build a strong nest to keep her and her chicks safely in the tree. Just like God gives the little sparrow a song to sing and wisdom to care for her young, He gives us wisdom, love and understanding to care for His creation and His creatures.

"Father made man a living soul and breathed into him His very own breath of life. Just as the sparrow passes on her life to her young, we pass on the breath of life that God gave us from generation to generation. As she is so small, compared to other birds, we are small compared to much of Father's creation but all things are under his watchful eye."

Mary was amazed. He always saw a lesson in Nature that pointed to His Father. She thought upon the way the angel Gabriel had come to her and announced that she had been chosen by God to bear His Son.

"How unworthy I am. How blessed I am. Truly God does not respect persons of wealth or fame but exalts the lowly that he might be glorified," Mary's thoughts spilled out into whispered words as they walked along.

After several weeks of walking, they caught sight of the beautiful, glistening, golden city of Jerusalem in the sunset.

CHAPTER 10
Jerusalem

§

ALL OF THE BUILDINGS WERE made of the same amber-colored stone that gave the city a golden cast.

Their hearts leaped with joy as they sang a Psalm together of praise to God.

They spent the night in Jerusalem with some old friends and continued their journey the next day to a little town in Judea to visit their relatives there.

When they arrived at the house of Mary's mother, they were greeted with squeals of glee as Mary's younger sister came running up the pathway toward them. She was twelve years old.

"Mary, Joseph, cousins...welcome home! Come on in, come on in."

Her dress flew above her knees as she ran and jumped. The chickens, that had been lazily strolling along the pathway scattered in every direction with loud squawks of terror at the sight of Sarah running toward them.

The tired family sat down in the house after the usual kisses and hugs of greeting from family and friends, as Mary's mother prepared some tea and hearth cakes for them.

It was a time of resting from the journey. It was a time of catching up on the news.

Jesus loved his family and excitedly exchanged stories about life in Egypt with his cousins and their stories about what was happening there in Judea.

Nevertheless, he longed to be alone with his Father and waited for the opportunity to leave. Jesus quietly slipped out from the crowded room and found a place nearby where he could be alone with his Father.

This was the rest that Jesus enjoyed and which he had longed for. During the trip, he had to stay with the family at all times. Now, he saw the chance to be alone with his Father. No one in the house noticed that he had left. Only Mary noticed, but she wasn't worried. She understands her son.

Later that evening, he slipped in and found a comfortable bed made for him in the corner of the room with the rest of his family who were asleep. Time was not important to him. He loved to be outside at night and gaze up at the stars and moon. He knew the constellations and stars by name.

Jesus lay down on the soft pallet on the floor, covered himself with a warm blanket and fell fast asleep.

The Passover Seder was kept in the same way and tradition as it had been handed down from generation to generation since the first Passover in Egypt.

Jesus left with the other children to find the hidden piece of unleavened bread. He never found it, but some thought he didn't really try very hard.

He listened as the elders recounted the story of the generations of hardship in slavery to the Egyptians and the miracles that were performed at the hand of Moses.

He knew the story backward and forward, and if anyone left out an important detail, he was quick to remind them of it.

After the dinner, family and friends gathered up their things and headed for Jerusalem where they would go to the synagogue to participate in the Passover ceremony. The men went to their designated area in the inner court and the women to theirs in the outer court of the temple.

Mary longed to return home once and for all. "How long will we have to be in exile? This wicked and evil king can't live forever!"

CHAPTER 11

The Wicked King is Dead

§

MATTHEW 2:19-23

AFTER CELEBRATING THE SEVEN DAYS of Passover with their family and friends, they packed their things, along with the delicious cakes and breads that Mary's mother had made for them to take along on their journey, and the carefully wrapped cheeses, eggs, and oils that Joseph's family had prepared for them.

They hated to leave. Mary hugged her little sister who tearfully asked, "When are you ever going to stop all this travelling and settle down Mary? I hardly know you. You've been gone so much. Besides, mama isn't well. I'll need your help to take care of her when she's too old to care for herself."

"Sarah, it isn't my decision to live in Egypt. The Angel of the Lord came and told us to go to Egypt for Jesus' sake. The wicked King Herod killed all the baby boys in Bethlehem hoping to kill Him. As long as Herod is still alive, we can't come back to stay. He would surely try to find Jesus and kill him." It was hard for Mary to hold back the tears.

"I'm sorry sis. I wish that old crazy king would just die. They say he has fits of anger, throwing things at people and everything. He yells, 'Make them stop crying!' I think he's going insane because of what he did in Bethlehem." Sarah's words touched Mary's heart deeply.

"God knows the number of his days and he will live only long enough to fulfill God's greater plan. We must be patient and trust Him to do what is best for all of us."

Mary's words reassured Sarah that God was in control.

"Jehovah has a plan that will be fulfilled and no one will be able to stop it."

Joseph called out, "Mary, where are you? We've got to get going. Where is Jesus?"

"I'm right here talking to Sarah, Joseph. Jesus is in the house with Mother. We'll be right out. Come on Jesus, let's get going. We've got a long trip ahead of us."

Jesus hurried outside at the sound of his mother's call. They each mounted their donkey with the saddlebags full of food and water for the journey. Mary's family stood outside waving goodbye to them as they started south toward Jerusalem.

After several hours on the road they noticed a man running toward them. "Look, he's waving something in the air. This must be important," said Joseph as he brought the lead donkey to a halt.

"The king is dead!" the man shouted. "The king is dead! Pass the word along! There will be a funeral tomorrow in Jerusalem."

The man paused only long enough to give the small family the news and then continued running.

"That's good news, Mary! We'll be able to return home now." Joseph was delighted with the thought of coming back home.

"As badly as I want to come home, we dare not leave until we hear from God." Mary's face was a bit sad and glad at the same time.

The return to Egypt seemed to take less time than usual. They only stopped to sleep and eat along the way. They had limited their stops to only the most necessary ones for themselves and the animals.

Upon arriving in the small town they had lived in for over ten years, they found that everyone knew the wicked king Herod had died. Horsemen had come throughout the area telling the people about the death of this evil king.

That night as the little family slept in peace with the rest of the villagers, God spoke to Joseph in a dream, just as He had spoken to him before when He told him that Mary's baby was conceived of the Holy Spirit, and like the time He told him to go into Egypt.

"After Herod died, Joseph had a dream while he was still in Egypt. In the dream an angel of the Lord appeared to him. The angel of the Lord said, "Get up! Take the child and his mother. Go to the land of Israel. Those who were trying to kill the child are dead." Matthew 2:19 (NlrV)

The Lord spoke to Joseph again in a dream and told him to go to the land of Galilee, to a town called Nazareth. (Matthew 2:23)

The Angel of the Lord told Joseph that he should return to Israel because those who sought His Son's life were dead.

The people of the town were sad to hear that Mary and Joseph were leaving to return to Israel, but nevertheless, offered their help in getting their things packed for the trip.

Some of the tools that Joseph used for his carpentry work were made of iron and were quite heavy.

They made a wooden cart with wheels and packed the axels with cooking fat. The long poles distributed the weight evenly so that the animals could carry the heavy load of tools and cooking utensils. They strapped it with leather strips and put the burden on the largest donkey to pull. They would not ride him because he would have the heaviest load of all.

With so much to carry, they would have to walk and rest the animals along the way.

The children from the village came to say goodbye to Jesus. We're going to miss you," they said with tears in their eyes. "Please come back when you can."

Jesus answered, "I may not be able to return, but I'll try, if God wills. I hope you'll never forget the things we talked about. We had a lot of fun together and I really enjoyed telling you about your heavenly Father, God."

At this, each of the children came and gave Jesus a farewell hug.

On the way out of town, Jesus stopped at blind Miriam's house.

"Where have you been my light and love? I waited for you to come every day!" Miriam's voice had a slight rebuke in it.

"Miriam, I came to tell you that I won't be visiting you any more. My family must return to Israel now. The wicked king Herod, who killed all the baby boys in Bethlehem, has died. It's safe for us to go home now.

"Please don't forget that the Father loves you. You are not as blind as most people who can see because you have found the light of faith. It fills your soul with hope for a future filled with God.

"Others are content with their lives and belongings and never give God a thought. They are filled with darkness where you are filled with light. Please don't cry. I love you. Never forget me or our talks."

A tear fell down Miriam's cheek as Jesus came and embraced her.

"I believe that I would sooner forget my own name than forget you, my Child." A tear fell from Jesus' eye too. No one had ever cared for her like Jesus.

Later in His life, Jesus would heal many blind and sick but this wasn't yet God's time to begin His miracle ministry by healing this blind friend.

Joseph and Mary's family had grown while they were in Egypt. Jesus now had some brothers and sisters. Because Jesus was the firstborn, he was expected to carry more responsibility than the younger children.

The town's people came out to wish the family well on their journey back to Israel. The town had been their home for many years and they had made many friends.

It was nearly midday by the time the little caravan got under way. The donkeys walked slowly behind Joseph, who led the lead donkey with a bridle strap.

The townspeople had gathered in the street to see them off. They stood silently watching as the last donkey disappeared behind the hill outside of town. This was the last time they would see Joseph and Mary and their children. The Bible prophecy of Hosea 11:1b (NlrV) had been fulfilled, *"I chose to bring my son out of Egypt."*

They started their journey but the mood was not joyful and happy as Mary had expected, instead it was somber. They were leaving the familiar little town that had sheltered them during the terrifying reign of King Herod the Great. The people of their village were warm and loving. The little family had brought with them the presence of God and the knowledge of the Scriptures, which they gladly shared with the villagers.

Faith was one thing they were leaving behind in the hearts of all those whom they had befriended. Even though the town was mostly gentile, they had come to embrace the truth of God's word that this little family lived daily, while among them. Many of them converted to Judaism because of the little Boy that knew God.

King Herod had not only murdered the children of Bethlehem but also his wife, three sons, and other family members. His death was a cause of rejoicing more than of sorrow.

Herod Antipater died and was buried with kingly ritual in Jerusalem, but his son, Archelaus, who was as wicked as he, ruled in his father's place. His mother, Malthace, warned her son that there could be an insurrection of the Jews since her husband had been so disliked by them. She advised him to be less lenient than his father and keep them in tighter control.

His son ruled for only ten years but carried on the family tradition of terrorism.

As Mary and Joseph entered Israel, they camped in a field to spend the night. That night Joseph had a disturbing dream. He saw a young Herod searching all of Judea for a child. He was being goaded by a witch who was telling him that he must find Him.

In the dream, Joseph heard a voice that said, "Do not settle in Judea but go to Galilee and settle in Nazareth. There the child will grow in favor with God and man and will become great."

In the morning, Joseph began hearing accounts from the shepherds in the fields where they were camped that this king Archelaus loved cruelty. He ruled by fear and terrorism. Fear gripped the heart of Joseph. He knew that the dream he had the night before was from God, like the other dreams that he had when God was leading him.

As he gathered up his tent and sleeping pallets, he was muttering a prayer under his breath, "Oh, great God of my fathers, Abraham, Isaac and Jacob, I thank you for guiding me at this time. Please protect us as we go and direct our steps."

"Mary do we have everything? Where is Jesus?" he called.

"Oh Joseph, you know He's not far, he just needed some time alone. He'll come running as soon as we start up." Mary answered.

Sure enough, Jesus came running across the field when he saw the family packing the things onto the donkeys. He had been playing with a lamb and was talking to one of the shepherd boys.

As usual, he had risen early and had his time of communion alone with his Father, then went over to play with the lamb.

"Jesus, this is no time to play! We have to be going! Don't make us wait," Joseph scolded.

"Yes, sir," Jesus replied, "I was watching and knew when to come. I'm sorry I made you worry."

The family traveled through Philistia by the sea route, stopping in Gaza for rest and provisions. Then they continued north-westward through Ashkelon and on to the city of Nazareth in the province of Galilee.

CHAPTER 12
Best Friends

§

LUKE 2:39-51

BECAUSE OF THE CONSTANT ROMAN intimidation, Joseph and Mary and the children tried to be as unnoticed as possible.

However, the wisdom and knowledge of this Child kept the elders and priests of the temple astonished and often speechless. It was not His time to be revealed but He was revealing Himself to them through the Scriptures, if they could only see.

When Jesus was twelve years old, his family went to Jerusalem for the week of the Passover, which was their yearly pilgrimage.

The whole family, including friends and distant relatives, travelled by foot for several days from Nazareth of Galilee to Jerusalem in the province of Judea. Even travelling in a large group such as this was not without its hazards.

The Roman soldiers would torment the travelers, demanding them to carry their equipment for them, compelling them to bow to their authority. It was the law that the Jews had to help the Roman soldiers for at least one mile. This was especially annoying since the Jews were not to have any dealings with the Gentiles. They were subjects of Roman authority which had little or no respect for the Jewish customs or religious beliefs.

As the group neared the town of Bethany, about two miles outside of Jerusalem, Joseph and Mary stopped to greet their friends, Matthew and Joanna, and spend the night there.

Their son, Lazarus, was always delighted when his friend, Jesus, came to visit. Lazarus had two sisters named Mary and Martha who were also fond of their brother's friend.

"Dad, can Jesus stay with us after the family goes on to Jerusalem?" pleaded Lazarus. "I hardly ever get to see Him and he's my best friend!"

"Tell you what son," his father answered, "they are going to be with us for one day, but if it's okay with his parents, maybe you could go with them to Jerusalem and then come back here with them on the return trip."

"Yippee!" shouted Lazarus. "Jesus, did you hear that, I can go with you to Jerusalem! We'll have a lot of time to talk and explore. It's going to be a couple of hours before dinner is ready. Do you want to go into the forest and do some exploring?"

He loved being in the forest with his friend. Jesus knew about all the animals and plants and when he was with him he had no fear of anything at all. Wild animals scared Lazarus but when he was with Jesus he was never afraid.

The animals seemed to love Jesus. They would quietly come over to Him as He stood still and they would beg him to stoke their heads and pet them.

Lazarus once saw an elegant stag come over to Him and meekly lay down at Jesus' feet. The foxes and wolves would come to Him as well as the tiny rabbits. In His presence there was no fear and the animals were at peace with each other.

Lazarus wondered about Him. How could he be so different? Wasn't he Mary and Joseph's son, or was he? Was He to be a great prophet or was he really the Messiah?

He just couldn't figure it all out. He just knew that the presence of God was with Him everywhere he went. Jesus was so different, but Lazarus loved to be with him.

"Lazarus, look at that beautiful butterfly! Its blue and gold gossamer wings carry it through the air from flower to flower as it sips their sweet nectar. It has a heavenly nature, but have you ever considered that it once had an earthbound nature?

"The old caterpillar nature had to die in order for it to take on the beauty of its heavenly nature. You might say it was born again. It's important for you to remember that, my friend," said Jesus thoughtfully as He sat down on a log, looking up at the fluttering butterfly in the sunshine.

They sat and talked and the time went by so quickly, that it was soon dark. "Uh, oh, we're in trouble now. We missed dinner and the forest is so dark we might get lost trying to find our way out." Lazarus knew that if he were alone that would surely be the case but not with Jesus.

"Don't worry. There will be food for us when we get there. I know the way out. Just follow me."

With that, Jesus arose and started through the darkening forest with Lazarus hanging on to the back of His garment.

They were soon in the clearing and could see the lights in the window of Lazarus's home. They had placed a lamp in the window so the boys could see the house clearly.

The following day they left for Jerusalem to keep the feast of the Passover.

They gave a sigh of relief when they arrived in Jerusalem for the week-long Passover festivities. It was a solemn yet joyful celebration to remember God's deliverance of the Jewish slave-nation from Egypt.

The Jewish people longed for a new liberation from their Gentile oppressors. When would the Messiah come and deliver them from this oppression? They were convinced that he would overpower and destroy their enemy, the Romans, and set up His kingdom in Jerusalem.

Jesus celebrated the seven days of Passover with his family and friends, but would slip out each day and go to the temple alone. In the temple, he talked with the priests and scribes concerning the Scriptures.

They were amazed. When they would quote the Scriptures to him, it had to be exactly right or he would correct them. They couldn't answer his questions concerning a suffering Messiah. They could only comprehend a victorious, conquering Messiah, who would rule the whole world and deliver them from their enemies.

"Tell us child," asked one of the Scribes, "who are your parents and where do you come from? You have such knowledge of the Scriptures, surely they have hired the finest teachers available to teach you these things. You are a very blessed child to have parents like that."

Jesus answered, "You say you know my Father, but you really only know about Him. He who created all the worlds created you and me and gave us His breath of life. Your life was passed on to you by your parents but God breathed life into Adam who passed it on to you. My life is from Him, just as yours is. The things which He created are the best teachers and examples of his nature.

"Don't you think that this is why the Gentiles know about Him, but they don't know Him?

"Why did God choose our fathers, Abraham, Isaac and Jacob to be lights of truth to His world? What did He mean when he told Abraham that in his seed all the nations of the earth would be blessed? "

The priest looked at this young lad approaching puberty. He was definitely a fine looking boy, but how did he come up with these difficult questions?

They simply looked at him in amazement and said, "Why don't you tell us?"

Just then Mary came rushing in to the temple.

"Jesus, where have you been? We've been looking for you for three days. We were worried sick! How could you put us through this? You know how dangerous it is to be alone here in Jerusalem because of the Romans!"

"Why were you searching all over for me? Didn't you know that I would be in my Father's house?" Jesus' tone of voice was not a rebuke but rather a matter-of-fact statement.

Mary just looked at him and embraced him in relief of having found her precious son alive and well.

Jesus returned with his family to Nazareth and lived there, working with Joseph as a carpenter. Then, when Joseph died, he and his brothers took over the carpentry business. They were skilled with their hands in all types of woodwork and were prosperous and blessed in the work of their hands.

People came from miles around to order furniture and other items from them.

However, his brothers could not depend on Jesus as he was gone as much as he was home.

He left the work of the carpentry business to them and spent much time alone in the mountains and by the streams of water.

His ministry was soon to be revealed to the world and his Heavenly Father was preparing him for a spiritual revolution that would change the course of the world.

CHAPTER 13

The Light of the World

§

JOHN 1:1-14, MARK 6:3

MARY KNEW THAT HER SON had to fulfill the Scriptures and never chided him for not helping with the business. When the others complained about him, she would defend him.

James complained, "Mom I don't understand. Why are you always favoring him over us? We have to do most of the work while he's out in the woods somewhere doing nothing! He does beautiful work, but he never seems to care if people like it or not. We all know he's your favorite, but we count too!"

Mary answered, "James, you have been a great comfort to me since your father died. I'm glad that you can carry on the carpentry business like he taught you. I know you resent Jesus because he seems to be uninterested in helping with the family income, but he has a destiny to fulfill that is far greater than either of us can comprehend. You, my son, and my other children are very dear to me. You each have your own life to live and destiny to fulfill. Don't worry about Jesus. He'll be exactly what God wants him to be when the time is right for him."

During this time, because of the reign of Herod Archelaus, the people groaned and cried out for God's deliverance. Archelaus was deposed as king after ten years of a reign of terror and another Herod took his place, King Herod Agrippa I.

Later, a man called John the Baptist, the son of Mary's cousin, Elizabeth and her husband Zacharias, was sent by God to prepare the way for the Son of God.

Elizabeth and Zacharias were descendants of Aaron, of the royal priesthood. Their son, John, of that royal Priesthood line would point out to the world that Jesus was the Lamb of God, sent to take away the sins of the world.

John came announcing that all must have a clean heart in order to be able to receive God's blessing and forgiveness. It was no longer enough to be able to buy a sacrifice to pay for your sins. You had to repent and be baptized as a sign of leaving the old way of life for a new way of life of commitment to God.

John the Baptist converted over a million people to the Lord who came to hear him in the wilderness.

Everyone was still longing for a Messiah that would deliver them from the hand of the oppressive Romans. But John the Baptist knew when he baptized Jesus in the Jordan River that this was the "Lamb of God" that would take away the sins of the world.

He saw the Holy Spirit descend from heaven in the form of a dove and rest upon Him. God the Father verified this when His voice thundered from heaven, "This is my beloved Son, in whom I am well pleased."

This Lamb of God was not destined for a throne until after He had shed his blood. His Kingdom is not like any other in the world. It is a Kingdom that transcends time, boundaries, and languages. No amount of persecution or hatred can destroy it or stamp it out. He is the cornerstone of truth that was rejected by the religious leaders of his day.

He became the ruler of a mighty Kingdom that has filled the whole earth with the glory and power of God. He willingly laid down his life on earth to take on His beautiful heavenly nature.

By so doing, He promised to never leave us nor forsake us. He sent His Spirit to come and fill our hearts so that we could carry on His work in our generation as He would have done if He were here in person.

There is no social, political, racial or age limit to receiving His life and power. All He wants is for you to come to Him as you are and receive Him into your heart. You don't have to change to receive Him, but He will change you if you do.

He told us that if we ask we will receive. John 1:11-12 (NlrV) *"He came to what was his own. But his own people did not accept him. Some people did accept him. They believed in his name. He gave them the right to become children of God."*

We receive Him by asking Him to come into our hearts. Why not do that now? He's waiting for you. Will you let Him be your Savior and friend?

"God loved the world so much that he gave his one and only Son. Anyone who believes in Him will not die but will have eternal life." (NlrV) John 3:16

This is a prayer that you can say aloud, and believe it in your heart:

Jesus, I believe that you are the son of God and that you died on the cross for my sins. Forgive me for all my sins. Come into my heart and write my name in the Book of Life. Fill me with the Holy Spirit so that I can live my life for you. Thank you. Amen.

EPILOG

§

GAMALIEL WAS SENT TO VERIFY or disavow the rumors of the child that was born in Bethlehem and that Herod tried to kill. According to the report that he sent to the Sanhedrim of the Jews Jesus was about twenty six years old when he went to find him. Page 92 of the Archko Volume book has a detailed description of Jesus, given to him by a priest that was often visited by Jesus. Gamaliel never saw him personally but due to all the reports that were given him by others he was convinced that Jesus was indeed the Messiah of the world.

REFERENCE MATERIAL

§

The Archko Volume
Keats Publishing, Inc.
212 Elm Street
New Canaan, CT 06840 ISBN: 0-87983-067-0

The Holy Bible
New International Reader's Version NIrv
Biblica ISBN:978-1-56320-591-0

Made in the USA
San Bernardino, CA
06 October 2017